Invisible

WRITTEN BY SUSAN PELTIER

DEDICATED TO TOM, ELI & LUCAS. I SEE YOU.

I AM SORRY IT TOOK ME SO LONG, MOTHER

"Believe in the impossible, because that's where the possible starts." – Susan Peltier

Part 1

Plates clinked next to the sink, where water roared as it hit the stainless-steel basin. The rich smell of tomatoes and basil filled the air, a reminder of the sauce simmering on the stove. Maggie, sixteen and the oldest sibling, moved around the kitchen with practiced ease. She adjusted the stove's dials with one hand while stirring the thick, bubbling sauce with the other, her movements fluid and confident, the steam rising to fog up the kitchen windows.

"Mom should be home soon," she said to herself, glancing at the clock on the wall. She felt a familiar knot of worry tighten in her chest. Preparing dinner often fell on her shoulders, a task she took on willingly but not without its pressures. She wanted everything to be perfect, to show her mother that she could handle things and lighten her load.

The phone's loud ring cut through the kitchen noise. She wedged the phone between her shoulder and ear without missing a beat. "Hello?" she answered, not taking her eyes off the saucepan. She tasted the sauce thoughtfully, then reached for the salt shaker to add a pinch more seasoning.

"Yeah, I'll tell her you called," Maggie said, her voice competing with the kitchen's background noise. She paused, adjusting the phone. "No, she's still at work. Listen, I've got to go. This kitchen's a disaster zone. Catch up later, okay?"

She hung up and got back to work, her focus unwavering. She glanced around the kitchen, taking stock of what still needed to be done. She moved with purpose, her hands a blur as she chopped vegetables, stirred pots, and adjusted the oven temperature.

While she worked, her thoughts wandered to the mountain of homework waiting for her after dinner, the laundry that needed folding, and the ever-growing list of chores. Sometimes it felt like there weren't enough hours in the day. She sighed softly, almost lost in the household noise. She wanted to make things easier for her mother, to be dependable, to show that she could handle the challenges thrown her way.

"I need to get everything ready before Mom walks through that door," she muttered, a sense of urgency creeping into her voice. Just as she lowered the flame under the pasta pot, the sound of footsteps approached from behind. She didn't need to look to know it was her younger brother.

"Hey, what's for dinner?" Sam asked, impatiently looking over her shoulder, "I'm starving."

She exhaled sharply, her focus briefly interrupted. She glanced over her shoulder, her expression a mix of annoyance and exhaustion. "Not ready yet, Sam. Can you give me some breathing room?"

He lingered a moment longer, drawn by the tempting aroma of the sauce despite her clear frustration. "But I'm hungry now," he protested mildly, his voice a soft whine.

She turned fully, hands on her hips. "Well, you'll have to wait. Everything's still cooking, and you being in here isn't helping. Go set the table or something."

He looked at the mess. "Why don't you help clean up a bit instead?" she added, glancing at the cluttered counters.

"It's not my mess," he replied defensively.

"Seriously, Sam? You live here too. Just help out for once," she said, her annoyance growing.

"I've got homework to do," he muttered.

"Oh, come on! I've seen you with that book all afternoon. You're just being lazy," she shot back, her patience wearing thin.

"Why should I clean up your mess? You're the one cooking!" his voice rose in frustration.

"Because I'm doing this for all of us! The least you can do is help," she snapped, her face flushing with anger.

He crossed his arms. "It's not fair! I didn't ask for this. You're not Mom, stop bossing me around!"

Her eyes flashed with fury. "If you're not going to help, then get out of the kitchen! Go sulk somewhere else if you're going to be useless."

He glared at her, his face red with anger. "Fine! I will!" he shouted, storming out of the kitchen and slamming the door behind him.

He found a secluded corner in the living room and collapsed into an armchair with a book. He flipped through the pages slowly, his fingers brushing the paper. His eyes followed each line of text, but his mind wandered, distracted by the everyday sounds filling the house. The clatter of dishes, the murmur of the television, and snippets of conversation created a familiar, comforting noise around him. These sounds touched everything except him, wrapped in his own bubble of solitude.

Bored, he wandered around the house like a ghost, his footsteps barely audible on the old wooden floorboards. He drifted from room to room, each one telling a story of a family drifting apart, the silence between them growing louder with each passing day. He paused in the living room, glancing at the TV. The dull drone of a game show didn't hold his interest. The bright colors and exaggerated reactions of the contestants felt hollow, a contrast to his own muted emotions. He remembered a time when he used to watch these shows with genuine excitement, cheering for the contestants and laughing at the host's jokes. Now, it all felt like a distraction, a way to fill the silence rather than something to enjoy.

He clicked through the channels, each one more uninspiring than the last. News channels with their endless cycle of bad news, reality shows with their manufactured drama, sitcoms with canned laughter that felt forced and artificial. None of it resonated with him. He longed for something real, something that would make him feel connected and alive.

He sighed, turning off the TV and letting the silence fill the room again. The house, once filled with life and laughter, now felt like a hollow shell, echoing with the ghosts of what once was. He passed the kitchen, where Maggie was busy with dinner preparations. The rich aroma of roasting chicken and herbs filled the air, but even that failed to capture his attention. He continued his circuit, finally ending up back in his room. He flopped onto his bed and stared at the ceiling, the ticking of the clock the only sound breaking the silence.

Eventually, the sounds of dinner being prepared called him back. He walked to the dining room, where the family was gathering. At dinnertime, he took his usual seat at the end of the table, feeling both part of and separate from the family chaos. The noise in the kitchen grew louder, with forks and knives clinking against plates and conversations overlapping.

Maggie was in lecture mode. "Sam, you need to get better at managing your time," she said, her tone firm. "If you keep procrastinating, you'll never get anything done."

He looked down at his plate, pushing his food around. His fork traced patterns in the mashed potatoes, a mindless distraction from the sting of her words. "I know, Maggie," he muttered, not meeting her eyes.

"Seriously, Sam, you have to plan better!" she cut through the chatter, sharp and authoritative. Her patience frayed from constantly picking up the slack. "It's not just about getting good grades. It's about setting yourself up for the future. You have to take this seriously."

He rolled his eyes, his frustration bubbling to the surface. "It's not my fault you think you have to do everything. You're the real masochist, Maggie!"

Their younger brother, David, looked up from his plate, wide-eyed at the escalating tension. "Why are you guys always fighting?" he asked, his voice small and uncertain.

Across the table, their mother glanced at them, her eyes tired but understanding. "Okay, you two, that's enough bickering. Eat your dinner. And, Maggie, maybe give him a break," she suggested gently. "He's a good student."

Maggie sighed, her shoulders slumping. "I just want him to do well."

Sam felt a rush of conflicting emotions. He looked at his mother and offered a small smile, more of a reflex than a feeling. He continued to poke at his dinner, the familiar sense of isolation wrapping around him like a shroud. No one seemed to notice his withdrawn demeanor, mistaken for shyness rather than the profound loneliness it was.

Inside, he felt a mix of anger and sadness. Maggie's constant criticism felt like a spotlight on his every flaw. Her words echoed in his mind, each one a reminder of his failures. He knew she meant well, but it didn't make the sting any less painful. He wanted to tell her how hard he tried, how much he struggled with feeling invisible, but the words never came out right.

His heart ached with a longing to be understood. He felt his family's expectations pressing down on him, making it hard to breathe. Every glance, every word seemed to reinforce the idea that he wasn't enough, that he was somehow less than what they hoped for.

David, the youngest, kept talking about school, adding to the background noise. "And then Mrs. Thompson said we're going to have a science fair!" he exclaimed. Sam felt another pang of isolation, feeling even more disconnected. He listened to the conversations around him, feeling like a spectator instead of a participant.

"Did I tell you about my new project at work?" Mother asked, passing the salad bowl to Maggie.

"No, what's going on?" David replied, his eyes wide with curiosity.

The topics jumped from recent school events to work gossip, none of which broke through Sam's isolation. Each laugh and shared joke reminded him of his own silence—a silence he wore not by choice but by circumstance.

"Sam, how was your day?" Mother suddenly asked, breaking through his thoughts.

"Boring," he mumbled, his response swallowed by the ongoing chatter.

"Wow, what a detailed answer," Maggie said sarcastically, rolling her eyes. "You're such a great conversationalist, Sam."

Sam's face turned red with anger. "Just shut up, Maggie," he snapped, glaring at her.

Mother shot them both a warning look. "Enough, both of you," she said firmly, the tension lingering in the air.

David's eyes darted between Sam and Maggie, his small hands gripping his fork tightly. "Can we just have one dinner without arguing?" he pleaded, his voice trembling slightly. His words cut through the tension, but the underlying discomfort remained.

Their mother, sensing the fragile atmosphere, tried to steer the conversation back to safer ground. "What would you guys like to do this weekend?" she asked, forcing a smile.

David launched into the discussion, his voice eager and animated. Sam watched him, feeling a pang of envy for his brother's carefree innocence. He wished he could be as unburdened, as untroubled by expectations.

After the meal wound down, the conversations shifted to evening plans. Maggie and Sam cleared the dishes, their interaction tense.

"Hey, help me with this, will you?" she tossed a dishtowel at him, who caught it with a reluctant sigh.

"Why don't you ask someone else for a change?" he muttered, his irritation barely contained.

"Because there is no one else, and unlike some people, I actually do my part," she snapped back, her eyes flashing with frustration.

He watched for a moment longer, then pushed his chair back. The sound of wood on tile was drowned out by laughter and clinking dishes. He stood, looking at the family scene before him—a picture he was in but felt apart from. Without a word, he slipped out of the room, his departure as unnoticed as his presence. In the hallway, his family's voices faded behind him, and he felt his invisibility settle around his shoulders again.

He left the dining room, the warm chatter fading as he climbed the stairs. His bedroom's cool isolation wrapped around him like a familiar blanket. He flopped onto his bed, the springs creaking under his weight, and the television's glow flickered across his face.

He grabbed the remote again and clicked through channels, each press mechanical. Bright colors and rapid scene changes flashed on the screen, but nothing held his interest for more than a few seconds. His eyes followed the images, but his mind wandered far from the flashing lights.

Hoping something would capture his attention and draw him into a world beyond these four walls, he continued clicking. Yet, as minutes turned into hours, the shows blurred together, a monotonous stream of sound and color. He lay there, a silent observer, unnoticed and untouched by the stories unfolding before him.

Part 2

The following night, his mother walked through the door and dropped onto the couch, her body sinking into the cushions. She closed her eyes, her breath heavy and slow. Her briefcase, papers spilling out, lay on the floor.

He saw her come in and quietly stepped into the living room. He sat down across from her, his eyes on her tired face, waiting for a chance to speak. He watched her for a few minutes, trying to find the right moment.

"Mom?" His voice was tentative, a soft intrusion into the room.

Her eyes fluttered open, her gaze cloudy as she adjusted to her surroundings. It took her a moment to register him sitting across from her, his presence both familiar and unexpected.

She sighed, rubbing her temples. "Sam, not now," she murmured, the fatigue in her voice making her words almost a sigh. "Please, I just need some quiet."

His heart sank. He had so much to tell her, so much to share, but he saw the sheer tiredness etched into her features. With a nod, he stood up, his disappointment heavy in his chest.

"Okay, Mom," he replied softly, his voice barely above a whisper. He lingered for a second longer, hoping she might change her mind, but the room only filled with the sound of her weary breaths. Reluctantly, he retreated to his room, his shoulders slumped, his expression folding into one of resignation.

The evening continued, the house settling into its usual calm. He stayed in the background, as unnoticed as ever. He began to understand that to be seen, he must stay hidden.

In the dim light of the evening, he sat curled up under the soft glow of a table lamp, twisting the fabric of his pants. The room was quiet, lit by the flicker of the TV and the low murmur of background noise. The silence buzzed in his ears, reminding him of his loneliness. His heart ached with a longing too deep for tears, too persistent to ignore. Tonight, he felt more invisible than ever before.

Suddenly, he stood up, courage rushing through him. The chair scraped loudly against the floor, announcing his presence. His usually calm face was now full of fierce determination. "I'm here!" he shouted, his voice cracking with emotion. "Look at me! I'm here!"

The living room erupted into chaos. Maggie's book fell to the floor as she turned, startled. The noise grabbed his mother's attention, pulling her from her tired reverie on the couch. She saw him standing there, his chest heaving, his eyes blazing with hurt.

"What is this, Sam? Why are you yelling like that?" her voice was stern, surprise and irritation sharpening her tone.

"I'm tired of being invisible!" he cried, desperation in his voice. "You never see me! No one ever does!"

The room fell silent. His bold words hung in the air. Her face hardened as she rose from the couch, her exhaustion turning into steely resolve.

"Sam, that is enough," she said, her voice low and controlled. "Go to your room. We do not scream and act out in this house."

"But Mom—" his protest was cut short by her pointed look, ending the discussion.

His shoulders slumped, the light in his eyes dimming. He turned away, his outburst silenced by his mother's words. When he walked toward his room, the colors of his emotions faded, leaving him feeling empty.

Mother watched him go, feeling confused and frustrated. Her heart ached briefly with guilt for being harsh. But the day's demands were overwhelming, and she thought her reaction was necessary discipline. She didn't realize her son's outburst was a deeper cry for attention.

The house returned to its usual rhythm, the incident quickly forgotten. He lay in his room, the door closed, shutting out both sound and emotion. In the quiet of his space, he whispered to himself, "I'm here." But outside his door, the world moved on, oblivious to his longing to be seen.

Part 3

Morning light filtered through the windows, casting long shadows across his hardwood floor. The house was unusually quiet; the rest of the family was still asleep, and the daily chaos had yet to begin.

He sat on the edge of his bed, staring at the small, worn backpack at his feet. Once used for school and playground adventures, it now had a new purpose. Inside were a few clothes, a water bottle, sandwiches packed with care, a flashlight, a pocket knife, a small sketchbook, pencil, some money and his favorite book. He stood and slipped on his jacket, the fabric brushing against his arms. Zipping it up felt like donning armor, a protective layer against the uncertainty ahead.

His heart pounded, adrenaline rushing through him. He felt scared of the unknown, the vast forest and the solitude ahead. Yet, he was also excited by the thought of adventure and freedom. He imagined peaceful moments, drawing under the trees and reading by moonlight, far from the pressure and feeling of being invisible at home. A recent argument with his siblings replayed in his mind, strengthening his resolve to leave.

He looked around his room one last time, taking in the familiar sights with a sense of finality. Model airplanes, awards, and a worn teddy bear stood as silent witnesses to his life. Each item carried memories of times when he felt both connected and invisible. His hand hesitated on the doorknob, doubt clouding his resolve. But the memories of feeling overlooked steeled his determination. The countless times he felt unheard and unseen pushed him forward.

He opened the door gently, making no sound. The hallway stretched before him, the familiar creaks of the old house bidding him farewell. With each step, he felt sorrow and liberation, moving towards an uncertain future. Outside, the crisp air filled his lungs with a sense of new beginnings. The dew on the grass sparkled in the early morning light. He walked with purpose, each step carrying him away from the house that never felt like home.

At the edge of the woods, the trees stood tall and inviting, their branches swaying gently as if beckoning him to follow. The scent of pine and wet earth filled his senses, a blend of freshness and decay that spoke of life and renewal. He took a deep breath and stepped into the woods, the light dimming as the canopy of leaves closed overhead. The sounds of home faded, replaced by the rustle of leaves and the chirp of birds. Here, in nature's embrace, he sought a new life where he could truly exist.

The deeper he went, the more the forest opened up, feeling like a whole new world. The trees formed a grand canopy above him, their branches twisted together like they were dancing. Sunlight peeked through the leaves, creating moving patterns of light and shadow on the ground. With each step, the leaves under his feet crunched, keeping time with his thoughts. The air smelled earthy and fresh, like damp soil and wildflowers. Tiny creatures rustled in the bushes, a hawk called out in the distance, and insects buzzed steadily.

His backpack grew heavier, not from its contents, but from the burden of his decision. Inside were remnants of hope—a sketchbook of landscapes he yearned to see and a small book of history that spoke of places and emotions yet unexplored. He marveled at the intricate details of the forest: delicate ferns, sturdy mushrooms and patient spiders spinning webs. The forest floor was a mosaic of fallen leaves, twigs, and vibrant patches of moss.

A growing connection to this place emerged. The forest seemed to breathe with him, its rhythms aligning with his own. The farther he went, the more he felt the forest watching him, acknowledging his presence in a way he had never experienced before.

Evening fell, transforming the forest. The trees loomed large against the darkening sky. The gentle swish of the trees as the wind whispered through them was joined by the far-off calls of night creatures. He paused by a large oak, leaning against it for support. Birds sang their evening songs, the wind whispered through the trees, and a nearby stream chattered over stones. These sounds, so different from the silence at home, filled the air with life.

His eyes opened, taking in the greens and browns of the forest. There was beauty here, and a promise of the new and unknown. His heart fluttered with excitement, but a pang of sadness tightened in his chest as he thought of his room, his family, the life he had walked away from. Would they notice his absence? The thought lingered, clouding his hopes.

Night deepened, and he found a sheltered spot beneath the canopy of trees. He spread out his jacket on the soft moss, creating a makeshift bed. The forest at night was both eerie and enchanting, the darkness filled with the sounds of life continuing unseen. He listened to the melody of the woods and closed his eyes, letting the sounds wrap around him like a natural lullaby.

Back at home, the usual evening chaos unfolded with one notable absence. His mother, coming home from work, called out as she put away her coat and keys, "Sam, dinner's almost ready!" She expected the usual silence, but felt a heavier, more pronounced stillness. Something was off.

She moved through the house, calling for him with increasing worry. "Sam? Sam, please answer me!" Each room was neat, undisturbed, and empty. The absence of her son grew more alarming with each passing moment.

Panic set in as she hurried outside, scanning the yard and moving instinctively toward the woods. "Sam!" Her voice echoed, desperate and scared.

The forest loomed large as she entered, the fading light casting long shadows. She stumbled over roots, her flashlight beam jerking wildly as she called his name. Occasionally, she saw a flash of movement, a shadow in the underbrush, but each time she approached, there was nothing. It was as if he had become one with the twilight.

Deep inside, he heard his mother's distant calls cutting through the forest's whispers. He crouched low behind a thick tree, watching the beam of her flashlight sweep by. He wanted to jump out and end this game, but fear held him back. Fear of returning to a world where he was seen but not truly noticed, heard but not listened to. Here, in the woods, he felt like he belonged. Out there, he was a ghost.

Her steps slowed, her breath coming in short gasps, not just from exertion but from the realization of her own neglect. How had she missed the signs? How had she let her boy wander so far? Tears blurred her vision, each step forward a mix of hope and dread.

She whispered his name, her voice barely audible above the babbling stream. "Sam, please," she pleaded to the forest, to the son she hoped to find. "I'm here now. I'm looking for you." Her tears fell into the stream, joining the flow of water, a symbol of her sorrow and her longing.

She stood up, wiping her tears, and continued her search with renewed determination. The forest around her seemed to acknowledge her presence, the trees parting slightly to allow her passage. She realized that finding Sam was not just about bringing him home, but about showing him that she had changed, that she was ready to truly see him.

Above, the first stars began to appear as the woods settled into the night. She felt the vastness of the forest, its depths unfathomable. He watched from a distance, his heart filled with longing and resentment, love and pain.

Night deepened further, and she made her way back to the path, defeated but not deterred. She would return, again and again, to look for him. Back home, she would try to mend what had been broken, clear the clutter that had obscured her view, and maybe, just maybe, learn to truly see her son—not as a shadow, but as the boy who needed her.

He remained in the woods, unseen but watching, invisible yet seeing everything. That night, both mother and son realized the depth of their disconnection, each learning in their own way the value of truly seeing and being seen.

He sat quietly on a fallen log, his legs swinging slightly as he listened to the faint echoes of her calls fade into the distance. Each call seemed softer than the last, swallowed by the vast forest. Eventually, silence reclaimed its hold, wrapping him in a familiar, comforting embrace.

The dark no longer seemed an emptiness to fear, but a space filled with life, subtly vibrant and pulsing with its own rhythms. The canopy above was a tapestry of stars peeking through the gaps in the leaves, their faint light casting a gentle glow.

Nearby, the fox he had seen earlier emerged from the shadows, its coat a soft glow under the moonlight. It approached him with gentle curiosity, its eyes reflecting a kindred spirit. He reached out slowly, and to his delight, the fox came closer, nuzzling his hand with its cool nose.

Behind him, a rustle in the underbrush announced the arrival of an owl, its enormous eyes wise and knowing. It perched on a low branch, tilting its head as if to offer a silent greeting. The creatures of the forest, once mere shadows flitting at the edge of his vision, now gathered around him, their presence a tangible warmth against the chill of the night air.

"I can stay here," he whispered to his new companions, a statement more than a question. The animals didn't speak as humans do, but he understood their assurances in the gentle touch, the soft calls, and the shared warmth. They offered him a place among them, a belonging he had craved but never found within the walls of his own home.

That night, under the canopy of stars and leaves, he felt a transformation. As he accepted the silent invitation of the woods, his form seemed to solidify from the shadows that had always clung to him. He became more than a boy who was overlooked; he became a part of the forest, seen and recognized by the community he found here.

The break of dawn, with its beautiful hues of pink and gold, filled him with a profound sense of gratitude. The forest had welcomed him. He no longer felt the loneliness that had once filled his heart. Here he was home. His journey had led him to a new understanding of where he belonged. In the early morning light, he sometimes heard a familiar sound—a voice calling out, filled with hope and worry.

Whenever he heard his mother's voice searching in the forest, he would sit with his friends, feeling safe until she faded away. Each call from the world he left behind tugged at him, but surrounded by his forest friends, he found his place.

He ventured deeper into the forest, grappling with a mix of emotions. The thrill of exploration was tempered by an underlying sadness. The isolation that had once felt like a prison now seemed to offer a strange kind of solace. Here, he could be himself without judgment or expectations. Yet, this newfound freedom came with a cost—a lingering sense of loneliness that gnawed at him.

He thought of his family, of Maggie's stern lectures and David's carefree chatter. The memory of his mother's tired eyes weighed heavily on him. Despite their flaws and misunderstandings, they were his family. The thought of never seeing them again left a hollow ache in his chest.

One memory that often surfaced was the day he left home. He could imagine the look of relief on his mother's face when she realized he was gone. He remembered her tired eyes, always focused on something else, never truly seeing him. He felt the sting of invisibility, the sense of being overlooked in a household where he should have felt safe and loved. Yet, there were comforting memories, too. He remembered the rare moments when his mother would sit with him and read a book, her voice soft and soothing. He thought of the times when Maggie would help him with his homework, her patience and determination a source of strength for him. And David's laughter, always infectious, always able to lift his spirits.

Over time, he grew and changed. He developed skills that he never thought he would need. He learned to read the signs of the forest, understanding the movements and habits of its inhabitants. He became adept at building shelters, foraging for food, and finding water. His hands, once soft and unused to labor, became calloused and strong. His perspective also shifted. He began to see the forest not just as a place of refuge but as a living entity, full of life and wisdom. He learned to respect its rhythms, to move in harmony with its cycles. He realized that his journey was not just about escaping his old life but about finding a new way to live, one where he could be both seen and understood.

As he lay under the stars, he felt a deep sense of belonging. The forest had welcomed him, and in doing so, had shown him that he was never truly alone. Here, among the trees and the creatures, he had found a place where he mattered. And for the first time in his life, he felt less invisible.

Part 4

Years passed, hidden among the whispering trees and dappled sunlight. He was at peace being invisible to the world until an unexpected visitor crossed his path one warm afternoon. He sat beneath his favorite oak, listening to footsteps crunching softly on the forest floor. A young woman with curious eyes and a hesitant step walked down the path he had traveled many times. He held his breath, used to being unseen.

Just as she was about to pass, she paused and looked directly at him. "Hello," she called out, her voice gentle.

Startled, he responded cautiously, "Can you see me?"

"Well, yes… sort of," she replied, squinting as if trying to piece together a puzzle. "I see your legs and arms, but your face seems to be, well… invisible."

A familiar pang of sadness touched him, and he nodded slowly. "Yes, I've always been invisible to the people around me," he admitted.

The woman stepped closer, her movements kind. "I'm Lily," she said, extending her hand with a warm smile.

He hesitated before taking her hand, the human contact unfamiliar but comforting. "I'm Sam."

Lily sat down next to him on the mossy ground. She took his hand again, more firmly this time. "Well, Sam, I would really like to see you for who you are."

Sam was curious about Lily's background and reasons for being in the forest. "So, what brings you here, Lily?" he asked, wanting to understand what drew her to this place.

Lily sighed, her eyes reflecting a mix of emotions. "I've always felt a bit out of place in the city. I work at a stressful job, and the noise and rush of everyday life just got to me. I needed a break, a place where I could breathe and feel connected to something real." She paused, looking around the forest with a sense of wonder. "My grandmother used to tell me stories about these woods. She said they were magical, a place where you could find yourself. I guess I wanted to see if it was true."

Sam nodded, feeling a kinship with Lily's search for belonging. "I understand. This place has a way of showing you who you really are."

Lily turned to Sam with a curious smile. "Could we go for a walk?" she asked, eager to explore more of the forest.

They found a small clearing, surrounded by wildflowers and the hum of forest life. Sam leaned back against a tree trunk, feeling at ease.

"So, you really live out here all by yourself?" Lily asked, her voice filled with wonder as she pulled her knees up to her chest.

Sam chuckled, nodding. "Yeah, but I'm never really alone. I've got more friends than you might think." His eyes sparkled with amusement. "There's a family of foxes over that hill. The kits are always sneaking into my camp to steal food."

Lily laughed, tilting her head back to catch the sun. "That sounds adorable! And here I thought my cat was a handful."

"The forest creatures are definitely more interactive than any pets I've had," he continued. He described his morning routines, how the birds woke him with their songs and how the deer watched him from a distance.

"And what about you?" Sam asked, turning the conversation toward Lily. "What's life like on the other side of the woods?"

"Oh, it's much less exciting," Lily replied with a sigh. "I live on the edge of the forest. I wake up to the sound of cars more often than birds. But I have a little garden where I grow herbs and flowers—anything that can survive my not-so-green thumb."

They shared a laugh, the sound blending with the rustle of leaves.

"I always wondered what it would be like to live surrounded by nature," Lily mused, looking around as if seeing the forest for the first time. "Coming here is like stepping into another world."

"It is another world," Sam agreed. "It teaches you about patience and the rhythms of life. Nature doesn't rush, yet everything gets done."

Lily nodded thoughtfully. "That's something I need to learn. Life back home feels so rushed. Here, it feels like time slows down, gives you space to breathe."

Sam smiled, grateful for the understanding between them. "If you ever need a break from the rush, you know where to find me and the fox kits," he offered.

"I might take you up on that," Lily said with a smile. "It's been really great, getting to see your world, Sam. It's beautiful here, and so alive."

The forest seemed to hold its breath. Gradually, as if the forest willed it, Sam's smile began to materialize, shy at first but growing clearer.

"Hi, Sam," Lily smiled, meeting his now visible eyes.

Sam felt a warmth spread through him, a connection he hadn't realized he was missing. He was finally seen, not just as part of the scenery, but as a person. The forest no longer seemed just a place to hide but a place where he could also be found.

They continued to talk and laugh, sharing stories and dreams. The forest around them came alive with the warmth of newfound friendship and the promise of more visits.

One afternoon, the quiet of the forest was pierced by a rustling sound. Lily turned towards the noise, her eyes curious.

"Sam," she called out, "Did you hear that?"

Sam, gathering twigs for the campfire, paused and listened. A few seconds passed before he shook his head. "It's probably just the wind," he said calmly.

Lily bit her lip, unconvinced. "Who could that be?" she asked, peering into the dense foliage.

"No one," he replied gently. "It's just us here. The forest makes all kinds of sounds. It's nothing to worry about."

Reluctantly, Lily nodded, letting her gaze linger on the trees a moment longer before joining him by the fire.

Later that evening, a faint voice drifted through the trees, a whisper that clung to the air. Under his breath, he muttered, "I wish she would go away."

Lily, sitting beside him by the dying fire, heard him. "Who, Sam?" she asked softly.

Sam sighed, staring into the flickering flames. "It's my mother," he said with a mix of resignation and sorrow. "I've always been invisible at home. She only notices me when she needs something or when I'm in trouble. It's like I don't exist unless I'm useful."

Lily listened, her heart aching for him. "Is that why you left?" she asked gently.

Sam nodded, the shadows of the fire playing across his face. "I left because I wanted to be seen by something, anything. I thought maybe out here, among the trees and animals, I could find a place where I belong."

Lily moved closer, wrapping her arms around him. "You're seen, Sam," she whispered. "You're not invisible to me."

The next day, sunlight filtered through the leaves, casting warm patches on the forest floor where they were gathering wild berries. Their laughter blended with the sounds of the forest when a hoarse voice interrupted them.

"Hello," said a woman, her voice barely above a whisper.

Startled, they turned around. The woman standing behind them looked weary and worn, her clothes tattered. Her eyes burned with desperate hope and exhaustion.

She looked at Sam, searching his features. Turning to Lily, she asked, "Have you seen my son? He was just a boy when he left. I've been searching for so long."

Sam's heart tightened at the sight of her, emotions swirling as he met her gaze, seeing the strain of years etched into her face.

Her eyes, familiar yet filled with tears, did not recognize him. He had changed, grown from the boy who vanished into the forest to escape the pain of invisibility.

Lily squeezed his hand, offering silent support. Sam took a deep breath, stepping closer to his mother. "Mother, it's me," he said, his voice steady despite the emotions inside him.

She blinked, her eyes focusing on his face, tracing the lines that time and life in the forest had drawn. "Sam? Is it really you?" Her voice broke with the question.

"Yes, it's me, Mom." His reply was gentle.

She reached out, her hand trembling as she touched his face. Tears spilled over, tracing paths down her cheeks. "I didn't recognize you... You've become a man," she whispered.

Feeling a rush of emotions, he took a step back to find his balance. Seeing this, she lowered her head, understanding his need for space and stepped away.

"I've changed a lot," he said, his eyes moist. "The forest has been my home. It's where I found myself."

She nodded, her gaze shifting between him and Lily. "I've missed so much. My biggest regret is not seeing you grow up, not being there. I want to see you now, Sam, if it's not too late."

She looked at Lily, seeing her in a new light. "And you must be a big part of his life," she said, extending her hand to Lily, who accepted it.

"Yes, she is. Lily has been my world here," he said, his voice filled with gratitude.

She smiled softly. "I am so grateful that Sam found someone who could really see him," she said. Her words were a poignant reminder of the time lost and the moments missed.

He looked at his mother, wanting to reach out, but couldn't shake the lingering reluctance. He never wanted to be invisible again.

Lily sensed his hesitation and gently squeezed his hand. He glanced at her, his eyes betraying a mix of uncertainty, fear and a flicker of hope.

A familiar tightness in his chest grew as his mother's words washed over him. He glanced away, his eyes tracing the contours of the forest that had become his sanctuary. Skepticism clouded his thoughts, the old fear of being overlooked surged within him.

"Mother," he began, his voice strained, "I hear what you're saying, and I appreciate it. But it's hard... really hard." He looked back at her, his eyes earnest. "This place, these woods, they don't just see me—they make me feel real, visible. When I was with you, I felt like I disappeared."

Her face fell, the joy replaced by a dawning realization of his fear. "Sam, I never meant to—" she started, but he raised a hand to stop her.

"I know you didn't mean to, but that's how it was. That's why I'm scared of going back to that. If you visit, if you come into this world I've made, I need to know you're here to see me as I am now, not to pull me back into being invisible."

The tension between them was palpable. Lily, standing beside him, reached over to squeeze his hand.

"Let's take it slow, okay?" he continued, his voice softening. "Maybe start with just a short visit. We can see how it goes from there. I need to protect this life I've built."

She nodded slowly, tears in her eyes. "Of course, Sam. Whatever makes you comfortable. I just want to know you again, in whatever way you'll allow. I see you, son."

She stood up, casting one last look at him, her gaze filled with sorrow and understanding. She turned, her figure slowly receding into the path that led out of the forest. As she walked away, the silence between the trees seemed to deepen.

He watched her go, he was clouded with feelings of relief and guilt. Relief that she respected his boundaries, and guilt for the pain he saw in her as she walked away. Lily, sensing his turmoil, stood beside him, her presence comforting.

Part 5

A few days later, Mother sat quietly on her porch, lost in thought. The world around her seemed unusually still, the only movement the gentle sway of the porch swing. As she sipped her tea, a faint, almost imperceptible sound caught her attention. It was distant yet distinct—a voice, or perhaps two, weaving through the trees.

Straining her ears, she finally made out the words, clear and joyful. "Mother!" It was Lily's voice, followed by Sam's, both carrying across the forest that had once separated them.

"I am here!" she called back, standing up as a smile spread across her face, her voice strong and hopeful.

"Come visit, Mother!" they yelled together, their invitation echoing through the trees, bridging the distance between them.

Mother grabbed her coat and headed toward the forest path that led to Sam's world—a world she hoped to become a part of, even if just for a visit.

She hurried along the path, but as she reached the forest's edge, her pace slowed. She approached the small, cozy home nestled among the trees. She saw him standing at the doorway, his posture relaxed but his expression holding a hint of cautious optimism.

Sam stepped forward and hesitated, hugging her lightly. It was brief, but in that moment, a silent acknowledgment passed between them—a recognition of past pains and a cautious hope for the future.

"Come in," he said softly, stepping aside to let her into his world. His voice was warm, inviting her into the simple yet charming space he and Lily had created together.

She paused at the threshold of the house, her gaze sweeping over the rustic beams and the cozy space. "This is lovely, Sam," she murmured, her voice filled with surprise and admiration as she stepped inside, touching the handmade curtains and smiling at the small collection of river stones by the hearth.

He, watching her reactions, felt a swell of pride. He spread his arms wide, encompassing the small but beloved space. "Let me show you around our home," he offered, his voice warm.

"I would love that," she replied, her eyes bright as she followed him.

They stepped outside into the cool evening. The fading sunlight cast long shadows across the forest floor. Lily pointed to a small garden patch she had started. "That's where we grow our herbs and some vegetables," she said.

"And over there," Sam added, pointing towards a cluster of bushes, "is where the foxes visit us sometimes. They're not very shy!"

She listened, her face lighting up with interest. "You've really made a life out here," she said softly.

Lily nodded, smiling. "It was tough at first, but we figured it out. Living here teaches you to be patient and respectful."

Sam pointed to a nearby tree. "See that oak? We call it the Giving Tree. We hang bird feeders there and leave treats for the animals. It's like a meeting spot for all kinds of critters."

Her eyes followed his gesture, taking in the sturdy oak with its branches swaying gently in the evening breeze. "It's beautiful," she said. "I can see why you love it here."

They walked back towards the house as the sky turned a deep shade of blue, continuing to share stories and laugh. "Do you remember when you used to take me camping?" Sam asked with a smile.

She chuckled, her eyes sparkling. "Of course! You always wanted to explore every corner of the woods."

"Those trips are some of my best memories," he said warmly. "It's part of why I wanted to live here—to feel that same wonder and connection with nature."

With each story, the distance between Sam and his mother seemed to shrink. As they approached the house, she reached out and squeezed his hand. "I'm proud of you, Sam," she said emotionally.

He looked at her, his eyes reflecting their deep bond. "Thanks, Mom. That means a lot."

Eventually, the sun started to set, and it was time for Mother to leave. She stood at the doorway, hesitating. "Sam, can I come back someday?" she asked tentatively.

Sam walked over and hugged her tightly. "Yes, I'd like that."

She pulled back slightly, looking into his eyes. "Can I bring Maggie and David next time?"

He smiled warmly. "Definitely. I'd love to see them."

She nodded, her heart feeling lighter. "Okay, I'll see you soon then."

He watched her leave, feeling a sense of peace and hope for the future. As she walked away into the dark, cool night, she knew this visit had changed everything.

Over time, what started as a brief visit stretched into days, then weeks, and even years. Each day strengthened their bonds, slowly weaving a new fabric of family ties, rich with understanding and acceptance. She adapted to the rhythms of forest life, finding peace in the simplicity and honesty of their woodland home.

As the seasons changed, so did their relationship; the past grievances gave way to a present filled with mutual respect, love and forgiveness. He, once a shadow in his own home, now stood solid and seen, part of a family that saw him, truly saw him, for all time.

www.ingramcontent.com/pod-product-compliance
Lightning Source LLC
Chambersburg PA
CBHW070947120626
46546CB00004B/1595